Time's Delights

Time is an unsolved puzzle that has fasci-
nated people throughout the ages. Poets
know that to understand something you
need to be patient and to 'stand and stare'.
That is why they don't try to define Time,
but to show it at work in the life of nature
and in the lives of all of us. Some poems in
this collection show the part Time plays in
our day-to-day living: they are about getting
up in the morning, catching a school bus or
putting off bedtime. Other poems show us
Time working slowly through seasons and
festivals, or still more slowly through history.
Yet others show the joy of a single, shining
moment of Time. But whether the poems
that follow speak with images of Eternity or
humbly record 'hours, days, months, which
are the rags of Time', they all express a
sense of the wonder and delight that we, as
Time's creatures, can share and enjoy.

R.W.

Time's Delights

Poems for all seasons chosen by
Raymond Wilson

Illustrated by Meg Rutherford

Beaver Books

First published in 1977 by
The Hamlyn Publishing Group Limited
London · New York · Sydney · Toronto
Astronaut House, Feltham, Middlesex, England

© Copyright this collection Raymond Wilson 1977
© Copyright Illustrations
The Hamlyn Publishing Group Limited 1977

ISBN 0 600 37128 X

Printed in England by Cox and Wyman Limited
London, Reading and Fakenham
Set in Monotype Imprint

Contents

Acknowledgements

The author and publishers would like to thank the following people for giving permission to include in this anthology material which is their copyright. The publishers have made every effort to trace copyright holders. If we have inadvertently omitted to acknowledge anyone we should be most grateful if this could be brought to our attention for correction at the first opportunity.

Barrie & Jenkins for 'To a fat lady seen from the train' and 'Night song' from *Collected Poems* by Frances Cornford

Mrs Bennett for 'Robin's song' from *Come Follow Me* by Rodney Bennett

Jonathan Cape Ltd and Mrs H. M. Davies for 'Leisure' and 'A great time' from *The Complete Poems of W. H. Davies*

Jonathan Cape and the Estate of Robert Frost for 'Stopping by woods on a snowy evening' from *The Poetry of Robert Frost*, edited by Edward Connery Lathem

Leonard Clark for 'Revelation' from *The Mirror*

Leonard Clark and Dennis Dobson for 'Fog in November' from *Four Seasons*

J. M. Dent & Sons Ltd for 'The return' from *Straight or Curly* by Clifford Dyment

J. M. Dent & Sons Ltd and Miss D. E. Collins for 'The donkey' from *The Wild Knight* by G. K. Chesterton

Dennis Dobson for 'Hallowe'en' from *Good Company* by Leonard Clark

Duckworth for 'The early morning' from *Sonnets and Verse* and 'Winter the huntsman' from *Selected Poems Old and New* by Osbert Sitwell

The Executor of the late Gordon Bottomley and Professor Colleer Abbott for 'Dawn' by Gordon Bottomley

Reprinted by permission of Faber and Faber Limited – 'Mid-country blow' from *The Collected Poems* by Theodore Roethke; 'O child beside the waterfall' and 'I never see the stars at night' from *To Aylsham Fair* by George Barker; Prelude 1 of 'Preludes' from *Collected Poems 1909–1962* by T. S. Eliot; 'Days' from *The Whitsun Weddings* by Philip Larkin; 'Weather ear' from *The Pot Geranium* by Norman Nicholson; 'Gale warning' from *Collected Poems* by Michael Roberts

Douglas Gibson for 'A memory', 'Mist' and 'January'

Mrs Nicolette Gray and the Society of Authors, on behalf of the Laurence Binyon Estate for 'O summer sun'

Michael Hamburger for 'April day: Binsey'

Harcourt Brace Jovanovich for 'Fog' from *Chicago Poems* by Carl Sandburg (© copyright, 1916, by Holt, Rinehart and Winston, Inc.; © copyright, 1944, by Carl Sandburg)

Rupert Hart-Davis, Granada Publishing for 'A day in autumn' from *Poetry for Supper* by R. S. Thomas

William Heinemann Ltd for 'Beech leaves' from *The Wandering Moon* by James Reeves

David Higham and Methuen for 'The dustman' and 'Intruders' from *The Golden Unicorn* by Clive Sansom

Mrs Ralph Hodgson and Macmillan London and Basingstoke for 'Time, you old Gipsy man' from *Collected Poems* by Ralph Hodgson

The Hogarth Press for 'Sleet' from *Measures* by Norman MacCaig

Ted Hughes for 'Autumn song' from *Happy Landings*, edited by Howard Sergeant and published by Evans Bros.

James Kirkup for 'Early rain' and 'Thunder and lightning'

The Literary Trustees of Walter de la Mare and the Society of Authors as their representative for 'The rainbow', 'No bed', 'All that's past', 'Gone' and 'The song of the mad prince'

Reprinted with permission of Macmillan Publishing Co., Inc. - 'The bird of night' from *The Bat-Poet* by Randall Jarrell; 'Something told the wild geese' from *Poems* by Rachel Field

Oxford University Press for 'Fireworks' and 'Giant thunder' from *The Blackbird in the Lilac* by James Reeves; for 'The Epiphany' from *Poems of Conformity 1917* by Charles Williams; 'The guy' by Robert C. Holmes from *Every Man Will Shout*, edited by Roger Mansfield and Isobel Armstrong 1964

Reprinted by permission of A. D. Peters & Co. and Jonathan Cape Ltd - 'Winter field' by A. E. Coppard

Laurence Pollinger Limited, William Heinemann Ltd and the Estate of the late Mrs Frieda Lawrence for 'Spray' from *The Complete Poems of D. H. Lawrence*

G. T. Sassoon for 'Everyone sang' by Siegfried Sassoon

Martin Secker & Warburg Limited for 'Last snow' and 'Prehistoric camp' by Andrew Young from *Complete Poems*, edited by Leonard Clark

The author's representatives and Sidgwick & Jackson Ltd for 'Romance' from *The Centuries' Poetry, Book 5* by W. J. Turner

The Society of Authors as the literary representative of the Estate of A. E.

Housman, and Jonathan Cape Ltd for 'On Wenlock Edge' from *Collected Poems* by A. E. Housman

The Society of Authors as the literary representative of the Estate of Richard le Gallienne for 'I meant to do my work today'

By permission of the late Mrs E. F. Starkey's Estate – 'A piper' by Seumas O'Sullivan

Hal Summers for 'Out of school' from *Out of School*, edited by Dennis Sanders and published by Evans Bros.

A. S. J. Tessimond for 'A hot day'

The Trustees of the Hardy Estate and Macmillan London and Basingstoke for 'When I set out for Lyonesse', 'Weathers', from 'A sheep fair' and 'The fallow deer at the lonely house' from *Collected Poems* by Thomas Hardy

Mrs A. M. Walsh for 'Bus to school' from *The Roundabout by the Sea* by John Walsh

Raymond Wilson for 'Midnight wood', 'Spring' and 'The traveller'

Mrs Iris Wise and Macmillan London and Basingstoke for 'The rivals' from *Collected Poems* by James Stephens

World's Work Ltd and Doubleday & Company, Inc for 'Meeting' from *Taxis and Toadstools* by Rachel Field

M. B. Yeats, Miss Anne Yeats and the Macmillan Company of London and Basingstoke for 'The old men admiring themselves in the water' from *The Collected Poems of W. B. Yeats*.

This happy hour

Leisure

What is this life if, full of care,
We have no time to stand and stare?

No time to stand beneath the boughs
And stare as long as sheep or cows.

No time to see, when woods we pass,
Where squirrels hide their nuts in grass.

No time to see, in broad daylight,
Streams full of stars, like skies at night.

No time to turn at Beauty's glance,
And watch her feet, how they can dance.

No time to wait till her mouth can
Enrich that smile her eyes began.

A poor life this if, full of care,
We have no time to stand and stare.

W. H. Davies

The early morning

The moon on the one hand, the dawn on the other:
The moon is my sister, the dawn is my brother.
The moon on my left and the dawn on my right,
My brother good morning: my sister, good night.

Hilaire Belloc

Pippa's song

The year's at the spring,
And day's at the morn;
Morning's at seven;
The hill-side's dew-pearled;
The lark's on the wing;
The snail's on the thorn;
God's in His heaven—
All's right with the world!

Robert Browning

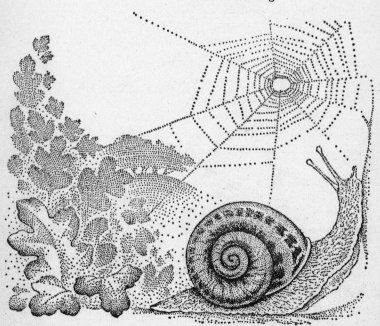

I meant to do my work today

I meant to do my work today –
But a brown bird sang in the apple tree,
And a butterfly flitted across the field,
And all the leaves were calling me.

And the wind went sighing over the land,
Tossing the grasses to and fro,
And a rainbow held out its shining hand –
So what could I do but laugh and go?

Richard le Gallienne

A great time

Sweet Chance, that led my steps abroad,
   Beyond the town, where wild flowers grow –
A rainbow and a cuckoo, Lord,
   How rich and great the times are now!
       Know, all ye sheep
       And cows, that keep
On staring that I stand so long
   In grass that's wet from heavy rain –
A rainbow and a cuckoo's song
   May never come together again;
       May never come
       This side the tomb.

W. H. Davies

To a fat lady seen from the train

O why do you walk through the fields in gloves,
   Missing so much and so much?
O fat white woman whom nobody loves,
Why do you walk through the fields in gloves,
When the grass is soft as the breast of doves
   And shivering-sweet to the touch?
O why do you walk through the fields in gloves,
   Missing so much and so much?

Frances Cornford

A change in the year

It is the first mild day of March:
Each minute sweeter than before,
The redbreast sings from the tall larch
That stands beside our door.

There is a blessing in the air,
Which seems a sense of joy to yield
To the bare trees, and mountains bare,
And grass in the green field.

William Wordsworth

from Auguries of innocence

To see a world in a grain of sand
And a heaven in a wild flower,
Hold Infinity in the palm of your hand
And Eternity in an hour.

William Blake

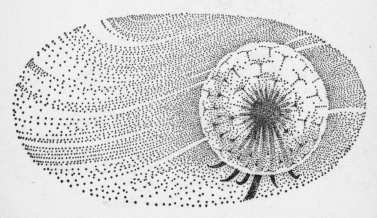

O summer sun

O summer sun, O moving trees!
O cheerful human noise, O busy glittering street!
What hour shall Fate in all the future find,
Or what delights, ever to equal these:
Only to taste the warmth, the light, the wind,
Only to be alive, and feel that life is sweet?

Laurence Binyon

O Child beside the waterfall

O Child beside the Waterfall
what songs without a word
rise from those waters like the call
only a heart has heard—
the Joy, the Joy in all things
rise whistling like a bird.

O Child beside the Waterfall
I hear them too, the brief
heavenly notes, the harp of dawn,
the nightingale on the leaf,
all, all dispel the darkness and
the silence of our grief.

O Child beside the Waterfall
I see you standing there
with waterdrops and fireflies
and hummingbirds in the air,
all singing praise of paradise,
paradise everywhere.

George Barker

Romance

When I was but thirteen or so
  I went into a golden land,
Chimborazo, Cotopaxi
  Took me by the hand.

My father died, my brother too,
  They passed like fleeting dreams,
I stood where Popocatapetl
  In the sunlight gleams.

I dimly heard the master's voice
  And boys far off at play,
Chimborazo, Cotopaxi
  Had stolen me away.

I walked in a great golden dream
  To and fro from school –
Shining Popocatapetl
  The dusty streets did rule.

I walked home with a gold dark boy
  And never a word I'd say,
Chimborazo, Cotopaxi
  Had taken my speech away:

I gazed entranced upon his face
  Fairer than any flower –
O shining Popocatapetl
  It was thy magic hour:

The houses, people, traffic seemed
  Thin fading dreams by day,
Chimborazo, Cotopaxi
  Had stolen my soul away!

W. J. Turner

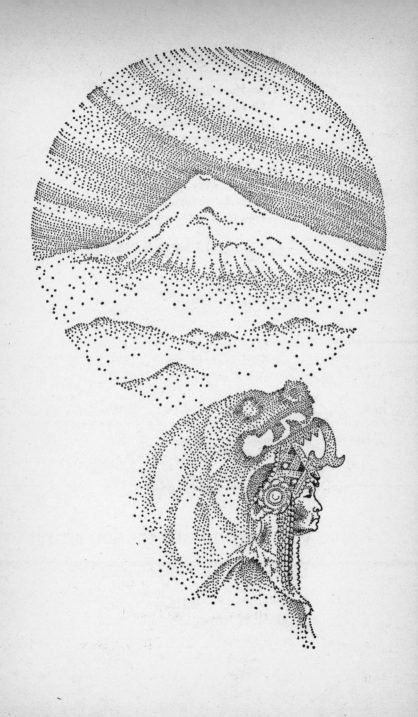

The rainbow

I saw the lovely arch
   Of Rainbow span the sky,
The gold sun burning
   As the rain swept by.

In bright-ringed solitude
   The showery foliage shone
One lovely moment,
   And the Bow was gone.

Walter de la Mare

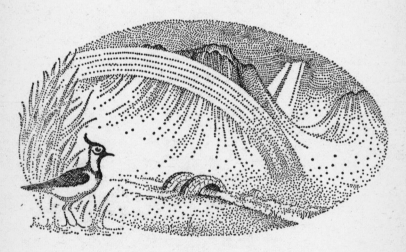

I give you the end of a golden string

I give you the end of a golden string;
   Only wind it into a ball,
It will lead you in at Heaven's gate,
   Built in Jerusalem's wall.

William Blake

Just listen

Just listen to the blackbird—what a note
The creature has! God bless his happy throat!
He is so absolutely glad
I fear he will go mad.

Thomas Edward Brown

Every one sang

Every one suddenly burst out singing;
And I was filled with such delight
As prisoned birds must find in freedom
Winging wildly across the white
Orchards and dark green fields; on; on; and out of sight.

Every one's voice was suddenly lifted,
And beauty came like the setting sun.
My heart was shaken with tears, and horror
Drifted away. . . . O, but every one
Was a bird; and the song was wordless; the singing
        will never be done.

Siegfried Sassoon

A memory

This I remember,
I saw from a train
A shaggy wild pony
That stood in the rain.

Where I was going,
And where was the train,
I cannot remember,
I cannot explain.

All these years after
It comes back again:
A shaggy wild pony
That stood in the rain.

Douglas Gibson

Adlestrop

Yes. I remember Adlestrop –
The name, because one afternoon
Of heat the express-train drew up there
Unwontedly. It was late June.

The steam hissed. Some one cleared his throat.
No one left and no one came
On the bare platform. What I saw
Was Adlestrop – only the name

And willows, willow-herb, and grass,
And meadowsweet, and haycocks dry,
No whit less still and lonely fair
Than the high cloudlets in the sky.

And for that minute a blackbird sang
Close by, and round him, mistier,
Farther and farther, all the birds
Of Oxfordshire and Gloucestershire.

Edward Thomas

A day in autumn

It will not always be like this,
The air windless, a few last
Leaves adding their decoration
To the trees' shoulders, braiding the cuffs
Of the boughs with gold; a bird preening
In the lawn's mirror. Having looked up
From the day's chores, pause a minute,
Let the mind take its photograph
Of the bright scene, something to wear
Against the heart in the long cold.

R. S. Thomas

Never till this happy hour

Many fair evenings, many flowers,
Sweetened with rich and gentle showers,
Have I enjoyed, and down have run
Many a fine and shining sun;
But never, till this happy hour,
Was blessed with such an evening-shower!

Henry Vaughan

A piper

A piper in the streets today
Set up and tuned, and started to play,
And away, away, away on the tide
Of his music we started; on every side
Doors and windows were opened wide,
And men left down their work and came,
And women with petticoats coloured like flame
And little bare feet that were blue with cold,
Went dancing back to the age of gold,
And all the world went gay, went gay,
For half an hour in the street today.

Seumas O'Sullivan

Revelation

At the midnight of the year
I saw them suddenly appear,
Ranks of angels in the sky.
In order they began the cry
Of 'Magnify, O magnify'
Above a shabby, northern street
Until their concord was complete.
But still the town's black work went on
Though over it all heaven shone,
Though every cobble was ablaze
And gutters running songs of praise.

Leonard Clark

I stood and stared

I stood and stared; the sky was lit,
The sky had stars all over it,
I stood, I knew not why,
Without a wish, without a will,
I stood upon that silent hill,
And stared into the sky until
My eyes were blind with stars and still
I stared into the sky.

Ralph Hodgson

Meeting

As I went home on the old wood road,
 With my basket and lesson book,
A deer came out of the tall trees
 And down to drink at the brook.

Twilight was all about us,
 Twilight and tree on tree;
I looked straight into its great, strange eyes,
 And the deer looked back at me.

Beautiful, brown, and unafraid,
 Those eyes returned my stare;
And something with neither sound nor name
 Passed between us there.

Something I shall not forget –
 Something still, and shy, and wise –
In the dimness of the woods
 From a pair of gold-flecked eyes.

Rachel Field

When I set out for Lyonnesse

When I set out for Lyonnesse,
   A hundred miles away,
   The rime was on the spray,
And starlight lit my lonesomeness
When I set out for Lyonnesse
   A hundred miles away.

What should bechance at Lyonnesse
   While I should sojourn there
   No prophet durst declare,
Nor did the wisest wizard guess
What would bechance at Lyonnesse
   While I should sojourn there.

When I came back from Lyonnesse
   With magic in my eyes,
   All marked with mute surmise
My radiance rare and fathomless,
When I came back from Lyonnesse
   With magic in my eyes!

Thomas Hardy

Whatever the weather

Whatever the weather

Whether the weather be fine, or whether the weather be not,
Whether the weather be cold, or whether the weather be hot,
We'll weather the weather, whatever the weather,
    Whether we like it or not.

Unknown

Weathers

This is the weather the cuckoo likes,
    And so do I;
When showers betumble the chestnut spikes,
    And nestlings fly:
And the little brown nightingale bills his best,
And they sit outside at 'The Traveller's Rest',
And maids come forth sprig-muslin drest,
And citizens dream of the south and west,
    And so do I.

This is the weather the shepherd shuns,
    And so do I;
When beeches drip in brown and duns,
    And thresh, and ply;
And hill-hid tides throb, throe on throe,
And meadow rivulets overflow,
And drops on gate-bars hang in a row,
And rooks in families homeward go,
    And so do I.

Thomas Hardy

The nightingale

On his little twig of plum,
  His plum-tree twig, the nightingale
Dreamed one night that snow had come,
  On the hill and in the vale,
  In the vale and on the hill,
  Everything white and soft and still,
Only the snowflakes falling, falling,
  Only the snow . . .

On a night when the snow had come,
  As the snowflakes fell the nightingale
Dreamed of orchards white with plum,
  On the hill and in the vale,
  In the vale and on the hill,
  Everything soft and white and still,
Only the petals falling, falling,
  Only the plum . . .

Ian Colvin
(From a Japanese Nursery Rhyme)

The owl

When cats run home and light is come,
  And dew is cold upon the ground,
And the far-off stream is dumb,
  And the whirring sail goes round,
  And the whirring sail goes round;
    Alone and warming his five wits,
    The white owl in the belfry sits.

When merry milkmaids click the latch,
  And rarely smells the new-mown hay,
And the cock hath sung beneath the thatch
  Twice or thrice his roundelay,
  Twice or thrice his roundelay;
    Alone and warming his five wits,
    The white owl in the belfry sits.

Alfred, Lord Tennyson

Glass falling

The glass is going down. The sun
Is going down. The forecasts say
It will be warm, with frequent showers.
We ramble down the showery hours
And amble up and down the day.
Mary will wear her black goloshes
And splash the puddles on the town;
And soon on fleets of macintoshes
The rain is coming down, the frown
Is coming down of heaven showing
A wet night coming, the glass is going
Down, the sun is going down.

Louis MacNeice

Mist

Subtle as an illusionist
The deft hands of the morning mist
Play tricks upon my sight:
Haystacks dissolve and hedges lift
Out of the unseen fields and drift
Between the veils of white.

On the horizon, heads of trees
Swim with the mist about their knees,
And when the farm dogs bark,
I turn to watch how on the calm
Of that white sea, the red-roofed farm
Floats like a Noah's Ark.

Douglas Gibson

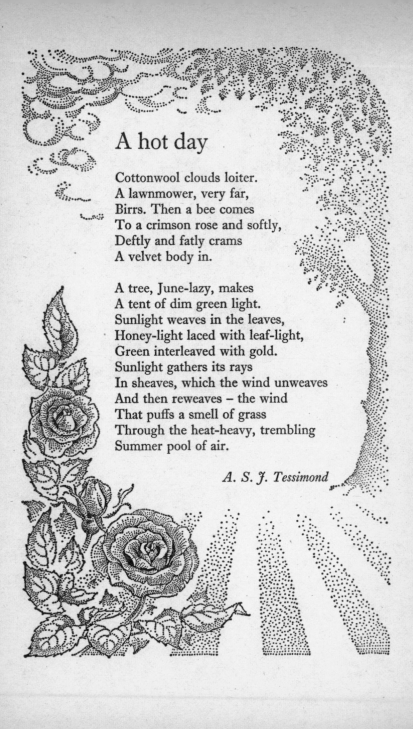

A hot day

Cottonwool clouds loiter.
A lawnmower, very far,
Birrs. Then a bee comes
To a crimson rose and softly,
Deftly and fatly crams
A velvet body in.

A tree, June-lazy, makes
A tent of dim green light.
Sunlight weaves in the leaves,
Honey-light laced with leaf-light,
Green interleaved with gold.
Sunlight gathers its rays
In sheaves, which the wind unweaves
And then reweaves – the wind
That puffs a smell of grass
Through the heat-heavy, trembling
Summer pool of air.

A. S. J. Tessimond

Early rain

After the long drought
The sun goes quickly out.
Leaf after leaf in the laden trees
Like cats' ears flick.
Dusty flowers on a dry stick
Stagger beneath the blows
Of the downpour breeze.
Each tree is a sounding drum,
And every rose
Is trampled in the hum
Of the shower's watery bees.

James Kirkup

Rain in summer

How beautiful is the rain!
After the dust and heat,
In the broad and fiery street,
In the narrow lane,
How beautiful is the rain!
How it clatters along the roofs,
Like the tramp of hoofs!

How it gushes and struggles out
From the throat of the overflowing spout!
Across the window pane
It pours and pours;
And swift and wide,
With a muddy tide,
Like a river down the gutter roars
The rain, the welcome rain!

H. W. Longfellow

Thunder and lightning

Blood punches through every vein
As lightning strips the windowpane.

Under its flashing whip, a white
Village leaps to light.

On tubs of thunder, fists of rain
Slog it out of sight again.

Blood punches the heart with fright
As rain belts the village night.

James Kirkup

from Summer storm

Look! look! that livid flash!
And instantly follows the rattling thunder,
As if some cloud-crag, split asunder,
Fell, splintering with a ruinous crash
On the earth, which crouches in silence under;
And now a solid grey of rain
Shuts off the landscape, mile by mile,
For a breath's space I see the blue wood again,
And, ere the next heart-beat, the wind-hurled pile,
That seemed but now a league aloof,
Bursts crackling o'er the sun-parched roof;
Against the windows the storm comes dashing,
Through tattered foliage the hail tears crashing,
The blue lightning flashes,
The rapid hail clashes,
The white waves are tumbling,
And, in one baffled roar,
Like the toothless sea mumbling
A rock-bristled shore,
The thunder is rumbling
And crashing and crumbling—
Will silence return nevermore?

James Russell Lowell

38

Giant Thunder

Giant Thunder, striding home,
Wonders if his supper's done.

'Hag wife, hag wife, bring me my bones!'
'They are not done,' the old hag moans.

'Not done? Not done?' the giant roars
And heaves his old wife out of doors.

Cries he, 'I'll have them, cooked or not,'
But overturns the cooking pot.

He flings the burning coals about;
See how the lightning flashes out!

Upon the gale the old hag rides,
The cloudy moon for terror hides.

All the world with thunder quakes;
Forest shudders, mountain shakes;

From the cloud the rainstorm breaks;
Village ponds are turned to lakes;

Every living creature wakes.
Hungry Giant, lie you still!

Stamp no more from hill to hill—
Tomorrow you shall have your fill.

James Reeves

If all were rain

If all were rain and never sun,
    No bow could span the hill;
If all were sun and never rain,
    There'd be no rainbow still.

Christina Rossetti

The rainbow

My heart leaps up when I behold
        A rainbow in the sky;
So was it when my life began,
So is it now I am a man,
So be it when I shall grow old,
        Or let me die!
The Child is father of the Man;
And I could wish my days to be
Bound each to each by natural piety.

William Wordsworth

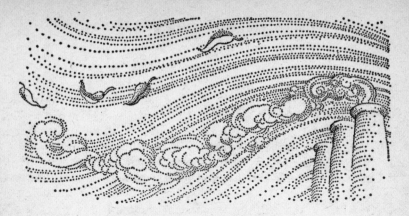

Chimney-tops

Ah! the morning is grey;
And what kind of day
Is it likely to be?
You must look up and see
What the chimney-tops say.

If the smoke from the mouth
Of the chimney goes south,
'Tis the north wind that blows
From the country of snows;
Look out for rough weather.
The cold and the north wind
Are always together.

If the smoke pouring forth
From the chimney goes north,
A mild day it will be,
A warm time we shall see;
The south wind is blowing
From lands where the orange
And fig trees are growing.

Unknown

Weather ear

Lying in bed in the dark, I hear the bray
Of the furnace hooter rasping the slates, and say:
'The wind will be in the east, and frost on the nose, today.'

Or when, in the still, small, conscience hours, I hear
The market clock-bell clacking close to my ear:
'A north-west wind from the fell, and the sky-light swilled
  and clear.'

But now when the roofs are sulky as the dead,
With a snuffle and sniff in the gullies, a drip on the lead:
'No wind at all, and the street stone-deaf with a cold in the head.'

Norman Nicholson

Mid-country blow

All night and all day the wind roared in the trees,
Until I could think that there were waves rolling high as my
   bedroom floor;
When I stood at the window, an elm bough swept to my knees;
The blue spruce lashed like a surf at the door.
The second dawn I would not have believed:
The oak stood with each leaf stiff as a bell.
When I looked at the altered scene, my eye was undeceived;
But my ear still kept the sound of the sea like a shell.

Theodore Roethke

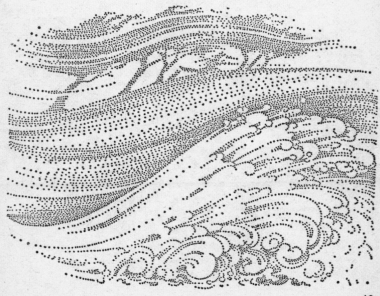

Winds

When the wind is in the east,
'Tis good for neither man nor beast;
When the wind is in the north,
The skilful fisher goes not forth;
When the wind is in the south,
It blows the bait in the fishes' mouth;
When the wind is in the west,
Then 'tis at the very best.

Unknown

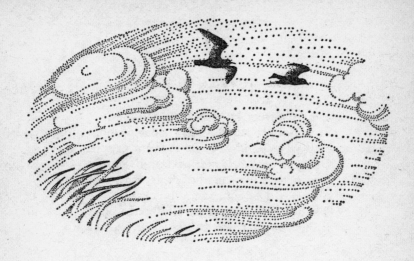

Gale warning

The wind breaks bound, tossing the oak and chestnut,
Whirling the paper at street corners,
The city clerks are harassed, wrestling head-down:
The gulls are blown inland.

Three slates fall from a roof,
The promenade is in danger:
Inland, the summer fête is postponed,
The British glider record broken.

The wind blows through the city, cleansing,
Whipping the posters from the hoardings,
Tearing the bunting and the banners,
The wind blows steadily, and as it will.

Michael Roberts

Fog in November

Fog in November, trees have no heads,
Streams only sound, walls suddenly stop
Half-way up hills, the ghost of a man spreads
Dung on dead fields for next year's crop.
I cannot see my hand before my face,
My body does not seem to be my own,
The world becomes a far-off, foreign place,
People are strangers, houses silent, unknown.

Leonard Clark

Fog

The fog comes
on little cat feet.
It sits looking
over harbour and city
on silent haunches
and then moves on.

Carl Sandburg

ROVER

from The song of the sea wind

How it sings, sings, sings,
   Blowing sharply from the sea-line,
With an edge of salt that stings;
   How it laughs aloud, and passes,
   As it cuts the close cliff-grasses;
      How it sings again, and whistles
      As it shakes the stout sea-thistles –
         How it sings!

Austin Dobson

Spray

It is a wonder foam is so beautiful.
A wave bursts in anger on a rock, broken up
in wild white sibilant spray
and falls back, drawing in its breath with rage,
with frustration how beautiful!

D. H. Lawrence

Sleet

The first snow was sleet. It swished heavily
Out of a cloud black enough to hold snow.
It was fine in the wind, but couldn't bear to touch
Anything solid. It died a pauper's death.

Now snow – it grins like a maniac in the moon.
It puts a glove on your face. It stops gaps.
It catches your eye and your breath. It settles down
Ponderously crushing trees with its airy ounces.

But today it was sleet, dissolving spiders on cheekbones,
Being melting spit on the glass, smudging the mind
That humped itself by the fire, turning away
From the ill wind, the sky filthily weeping.

Norman MacCaig

Snow

Out of the bosom of the air,
Out of the cloudfolds of her garments shaken,
Over the woodlands, brown and bare,
Over the harvest-fields forsaken,
Silent, and soft, and slow
Descends the snow.

H. W. Longfellow

from Snow storm

What a night! The wind howls, hisses, and but stops
To howl more loud, while the snow volley keeps
Incessant batter at the window pane,
Making our comfort feel as sweet again;
And in the morning, when the tempest drops,
At every cottage door mountainous heaps
Of snow lie drifted, that all entrance stops
Until the besom and the shovel gain
The path, and leave a wall on either side.

John Clare

Snow

In the gloom of whiteness,
In the great silence of snow,
A child was sighing
And bitterly saying: 'Oh,
They have killed a white bird up there on her nest,
The down is fluttering from her breast!'
And still it fell through the dusky brightness
On the child crying for the bird of the snow.

Edward Thomas

Morning, noon and night

A morning song

Morning has broken
Like the first morning,
Blackbird has spoken
Like the first bird.
Praise for the singing!
Praise for the morning!
Praise for them, springing
From the First Word!

Sweet the rain's new fall
Sunlit from heaven,
Like the first dewfall
On the first grass.
Praise for the sweetness
Of the wet garden,
Sprung in completeness
Where his feet pass.

Mine is the sunlight!
Mine is the morning
Born of the one light
Eden saw play!
Praise with elation,
Praise every morning,
God's re-creation
Of the new day!

Eleanor Farjeon

Hark, hark! the lark

Hark, hark! The lark at heaven's gate sings
    And Phoebus 'gins arise,
His steeds to water at those springs
    On chaliced flowers that lies;
And winking mary-buds begin
    To ope their golden eyes;
With everything that pretty is,
    My lady, sweet, arise:
        Arise, arise!

William Shakespeare

from His grange

        Though clock,
To tell how night draws hence, I've none,
        A cock
I have to sing how day draws on . . .

Robert Herrick

Dawn

The thrush is tapping a stone
With a snail's shell in its beak;
A small bird hangs from a cherry
Until the stem shall break.
No waking song has begun,
And yet birds chatter and hurry
And throng in the elm's gloom,
Because an owl goes home.

Gordon Bottomley

The rivals

I heard a bird at dawn
  Singing sweetly on a tree,
That the dew was on the lawn,
  And the wind was on the lea!
But I didn't listen to him,
  For he didn't sing to me!

I didn't listen to him,
  For he didn't sing to me
That the dew was on the lawn,
  And the wind was on the lea!
I was singing all the time
  Just as prettily as he!

I was singing all the time,
  Just as prettily as he,
About the dew upon the lawn,
  And the wind upon the lea!
So I didn't listen to him
  As he sang upon a tree!

James Stephens

Morning after a storm

There was a roaring in the wind all night;
The rain came heavily and fell in floods;
But now the sun is rising calm and bright;
The birds are singing in the distant woods;
Over his own sweet voice the stock-dove broods;
The Jay makes answer as the Magpie chatters;
And all the air is filled with pleasant noise of waters.

All things that love the sun are out of doors;
The sky rejoices in the morning's birth;
The grass is bright with rain-drops – on the moors
The hare is running races in her mirth;
And with her feet she from the plashy earth
Raises a mist, that, glittering in the sun,
Runs with her all the way, wherever she doth run.

William Wordsworth

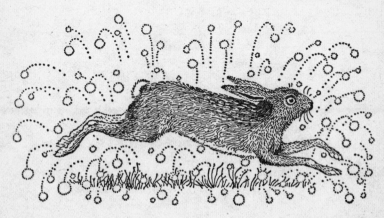

Noon

The midday hour of twelve the clock counts o'er,
   A sultry stillness lulls the air asleep;
The very buzz of flies is heard no more,
   Nor faintest wrinkles o'er the waters creep.
Like one large sheet of glass the pool does shine,
   Reflecting in its face the burnt sunbeam:
The very fish their sturting play decline,
   Seeking the willow shadows 'side the stream.
And, where the hawthorn branches o'er the pool,
   The little bird, forsaking song and nest,
Flutters on dripping twigs his limbs to cool,
   And splashes in the stream his burning breast.
Oh, free from thunder, for a sudden shower,
To cherish nature in this noonday hour!

John Clare

Noontide heat

A silence of full noontide heat
Grew on them at their toil:
The farmer's dog woke up from sleep,
The green snake hid her coil
Where grass grew thickest; bird and beast
Sought shadows as they could,
The reaping men and women paused
And sat down where they stood;
They ate and drank and were refreshed,
For rest from toil is good.

Christina Rossetti

from Summer evening

Crows crowd croaking overhead,
Hastening to the woods to bed.
Cooing sits the lonely dove,
Calling home her absent love.
With 'Kirchup! Kirchup!' 'mong the wheats,
Partridge distant partridge greets. . . .

Bats flit by in hood and cowl;
Through the barn-hole pops the owl;
From the hedge, in drowsy hum,
Heedless buzzing beetles bum,
Haunting every bushy place,
Flopping in the labourer's face. . . .

John Clare

Sunset

The summer sun is sinking low;
  Only the tree-tops redden and glow;
Only the weather-cock on the spire
Of the village church is a flame of fire;
  All is in shadow below.

H. W. Longfellow

The darkening garden

Where have all the colours gone?

Red of roses, green of grass,
Brown of tree-trunk, gold of cowslip,
Pink of poppy, blue of cornflower,
Who among you saw them pass?

They have gone to make the sunset:

Broidered on the western sky,
All the colours of our garden,
Woven into a lovely curtain,
Over the bed where Day doth die.

Unknown

The warning

Just now,
Out of the strange
Still dusk ... as strange as still ...
A white moth flew.
Why am I grown so cold?

Adelaide Crapsey

Evening

The sun is set; the swallows are asleep;
The bats are flitting fast in the grey air;
The slow soft toads out of damp corners creep,
And evening's breath, wandering here and there
Over the quivering surface of the stream,
Wakes not one ripple from its summer dream.

Percy Bysshe Shelley

Intruder

The sun only scorches,
It doesn't watch; but the moon watches.
He peers down low at the earth
As we cross his path;
He fills the unmoving meadows
With white light and dark moon-shadows;
He stares into my room as far as he can reach,
Like a man with a large torch.

Clive Sansom

Night song

On moony nights the dogs bark shrill
Down the valley and up the hill.

There's one who is angry to behold
The moon so unafraid and cold,
That makes the earth as bright as day,
But yet unhappy, dead, and grey.

Another in his strawy lair,
Says: 'Who's a-howling over there?
By heavens I will stop him soon
From interfering with the moon.'

So back he barks, with throat upthrown;
'You leave our moon, our moon alone.'
And other distant dogs respond
Beyond the fields, beyond, beyond.

Frances Cornford

The bird of night

A shadow is floating through the moonlight.
Its wings don't make a sound.
Its claws are long, its beak is bright.
Its eyes try all the corners of the night.

It calls and calls: all the air swells and heaves
And washes up and down like water.
The ear that listens to the owl believes
In death. The bat beneath the eaves,

The mouse beside the stone are still as death.
The owl's air washes them like water.
The owl goes back and forth inside the night,
And the night holds its breath.

Randall Jarrell

Moonlight, summer moonlight

'Tis moonlight, summer moonlight,
   All soft and still and fair;
The silent time of midnight
   Shines sweetly everywhere,

But most where trees are sending
   Their breezy boughs on high,
Or stooping low are lending
   A shelter from the sky.

Emily Brontë

I never see the stars at night

I never see the stars at night
    waltzing round the Moon
without wondering why they dance when
    no one plays a tune.

I hear no fiddles in the air
    or high and heavenly band
but round about they dance, the stars
    for ever hand in hand.

I think that wise ventriloquist
    the Old Man in the Moon
whistles so that only stars
    can hear his magic tune.

George Barker

Street scene

In the placid summer midnight,
    Under the drowsy sky,
I seem to hear in the stillness
    The moths go glimmering by.

One by one from the windows
    The lights have all been sped,
Never a blind looks conscious—
    The street is asleep in bed!

W. H. Henley

Noises in the night

Midnight's bell goes ting, ting, ting, ting, ting,
Then dogs do howl, and not a bird does sing
But the nightingale, and she goes twit, twit, twit,
Owls then on every bough do sit,
Ravens croak on chimney tops,
The cricket in the chamber hops,
And the cats cry mew, mew, mew.
The nibbling mouse is not asleep,
But he goes peep, peep, peep, peep, peep.
    And the cats cry mew, mew, mew,
    And still the cats cry mew, mew, mew.

Thomas Middleton

The night will never stay

The night will never stay,
  The night will still go by,
Though with a million stars
  You pin it to the sky,
Though you bind it with the blowing wind
  And buckle it with the moon,
The night will slip away
  Like sorrow or a tune.

Eleanor Farjeon

Midnight wood

Dark in the wood the shadows stir:
    What do you see? –
Mist and moonlight, star and cloud,
Hunchback shapes that creep and crowd
    From tree to tree.

Dark in the wood a thin wind calls:
    What do you hear? –
Frond and fern and clutching grass
Snigger at you as you pass,
    Whispering fear.

Dark in the wood a river flows:
    What does it hide? –
Otter, water-rat, old tin can,
Bones of fish and bones of a man
    Drift in its tide.

Dark in the wood the owlets shriek:
    What do they cry? –
Choose between the wood and river;
Who comes here is lost forever,
    And must die!

Raymond Wilson

All in a day

Days

What are days for?
Days are where we live.
They come, they wake us
Time and time over.
They are to be happy in:
Where can we live but days?

Ah, solving that question
Brings the priest and the doctor
In their long coats
Running over the fields.

Philip Larkin

Monday's child

Monday's child is fair of face,
Tuesday's child is full of grace,
Wednesday's child is full of woe,
Thursday's child has far to go,
Friday's child is loving and giving,
Saturday's child works hard for a living,
But the child that is born on the Sabbath day
Is bonny, and blithe, and good, and gay.

Unknown

Sister, awake

Sister, awake! close not your eyes.
 The day her light discloses,
And the bright morning doth arise
 Out of her bed of roses.

See the clear sun, the world's bright eye,
 In at our window peeping:
Lo, how he blusheth to espy
 Us idle wenches sleeping!

Therefore awake! make haste, I say,
 And let us, without staying,
All in our gowns of green so gay
 Into the park a-maying.

Unknown

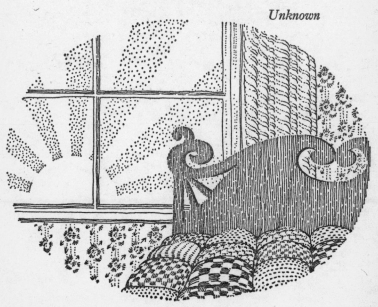

The dustman

Every Thursday morning
Before we're quite awake,
Without the slightest warning
The house begins to shake
    With a Biff! Bang!
    Biff! Bang! Biff!
It's the Dustman, who begins
    (BANG! CRASH!)
To empty all the bins
Of their rubbish and their ash
    With a Biff! Bang!
    Biff! Bang! Crash!

Clive Sansom

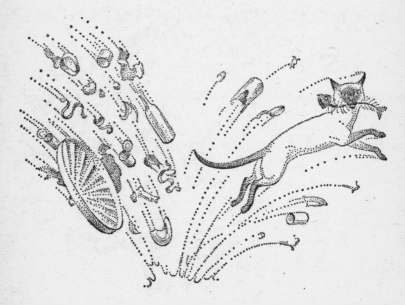

Up in the morning

Up in the morning's no for me,
  Up in the morning early;
When a' the hills are covered wi' snaw,
  I'm sure it's winter fairly.

Cauld blaws the wind frae east to west,
  The drift is driving sairly;
Sae loud and shrill I hear the blast,
  I'm sure it's winter sairly.

Up in the morning's no for me,
  Up in the morning early;
When a' the hills are covered wi' snaw,
  I'm sure it's winter fairly.

The birds sit chittering in the thorn,
  A' day they fare but sparely;
And long's the night frae even to morn,
  I'm sure it's winter fairly.

Up in the morning's no for me,
  Up in the morning early;
When a' the hills are covered wi' snaw,
  I'm sure it's winter fairly.

Robert Burns

'Bus to school

Rounding the corner
It comes to a stay.
Quick! Grab a rail!
Now we're off on our way . . .
Oh, but it's Thursday
The day of fear!
Three hateful lessons!
And school draws near.

Here in the 'bus though
There's plenty to see:
Boys full of talk about
Last night's T.V.;
Girls with their violins,
Armfuls of twigs
And flowers for teacher;
Bartlett and Biggs;
Conductor who chats with them,
Jokes about cricket;
Machine that flicks out
A white ribbon of ticket . . .
Yes, but it's Thursday,
The day of fear! –
Six hateful lessons!
And school draws near.

Conductor now waiting,
Firm as a rock,
For Billy whose penny's
Slid down in his sock.
Conductor frowning,
Hand on his handle;
Poor Billy blushes,
Undoes his sandal . . .
'Hold very tight, please,
Any more fares?'
Whistling conductor
Goes clumping upstairs . . .
Boots up above now!
Boys coming down! . . .
Over the hump-bridge
And into the town.

Old Warren sweeping
In his shirt-sleeves!
Sun on his shop-front,
Sun on the leaves . . .
Only, it's Thursday,
The day of fear!
All hateful lessons!
And school draws near.

John Walsh

School bell

Nine-o'Clock Bell!
Nine-o'Clock Bell!
All the small children and big ones as well,
Pulling their stockings up, snatching their hats,
Cheeking and grumbling and giving back-chats,
Laughing and quarrelling, dropping their things,
These at a snail's pace and those upon wings,
Lagging behind a bit, running ahead,
Waiting at corners for lights to turn red,
Some of them scurrying,
Others not worrying,
Carelessly trudging or anxiously hurrying,
All through the streets they are coming pell-mell
At the Nine-o'Clock
Nine-o'Clock
Nine-o'Clock
Bell!

Eleanor Farjeon

School dinners

If you stay to school dinners
Better throw them aside;
A lot of kids didn't,
A lot of kids died.

The meat is made of iron,
The spuds are made of steel;
And if that don't get you
The afters will!

Unknown

Out of school

Four o'clock strikes,
There's a rising hum,
Then the doors fly open,
The children come.

With a wild cat-call
And a hop-scotch hop
And a bouncing ball
And a whirling top,

Grazing of knees,
A hair pull and a slap,
A hitched-up satchel,
A pulled-down cap,

Bully boys reeling off,
Hurt ones squealing off,
Aviators wheeling off,
Mousy ones stealing off,
Woollen gloves for chilblains,
Cotton rags for snufflers,
Pigtails, coat-tails,
Tails of mufflers,

Machinegun cries,
A kennelful of snarlings,
A hurricane of leaves,
A treeful of starlings,

Thinning away now
By some and some,
Thinning away, away,
All gone home.

Hal Summers

Evening schoolboys

Hark to that happy shout! – the school-house door
  Is open thrown, and out the younkers teem;
Some run to leap-frog on the rushy moor,
  And others dabble in the shallow stream,
Catching young fish, and turning pebbles o'er
  For mussel-clams. Look in that mellow gleam,
Where the retiring sun, that rests the while,
  Streams through the broken hedge! How happy seem
Those friendly schoolboys leaning o'er the stile,
  Both reading in one book! – Anon a dream,
Rich with new joys, doth their young hearts beguile,
  And the book's pocketed right hastily.
Ah, happy boys! well may ye turn and smile,
  When joys are yours that never cost a sigh.

John Clare

The moon doth shine

Girls and boys come out to play,
The moon doth shine as bright as day;
Leave your supper and leave your sleep,
And come with your playfellows in the street;
Come with a whoop and come with a call,
Come with a goodwill or not at all.
Up the ladder and down the wall,
A halfpenny roll will serve us all.
You find milk and I'll find flour,
And we'll make a pudding in half an hour.

Unknown

No bed

No bed! no bed! we shouted,
And wheeled our eyes from home
To where the green and golden woods
      Cried, Come!

Wild sang the evening birds,
The sun-clouds shone in our eyes,
A silver snippet of moon hung low
      In the skies.

We ran, we leapt, we sang,
We yodelled loud and shrill,
Chased Nobody through the valley and
      Up the hill.

We laughed, we quarrelled, we drank
The cool sweet of the dew,
Beading on bud and leaf the dim
      Woods through.

We stayed, we listened, we looked –
Now dark was on the prowl!
Too-whit-a-woo, from its hollow called
      An owl. . . .

O Sleep, at last to slide
Into eyes made drunk with light;
Call in thy footsore boys to harmless
      Night!

Walter de la Mare

from Night

The sun descending in the west,
The evening star does shine;
The birds are silent in their nest,
And I must seek for mine.
The moon, like a flower,
In heaven's high bower,
With silent delight
Sits and smiles on the night.

William Blake

The return

The key turns in the lock,
And I enter my room.
I can hear the solemn clock
Being bold in the gloom.

Through the dark pane
Comes the moon's light,
But it does not explain
The secret way of night.

Only strange shapes
I can see:
The evening drapes
Rooms with black sorcery.

Pausing for light, I can hear
The clock, in the gloom,
Talking to the queer
Ghost in my room.

Clifford Dyment

The hag

The Hag is astride,
   This night for to ride;
The Devil and she together:
   Through thick and through thin,
   Now out and then in,
Though never so foul be the weather.

   A thorn or a burr
   She takes for a spur:
With a lash of a bramble she rides now,
   Through brakes and through briars,
   Over ditches and mires,
She follows the Spirit that guides now.

   No Beast, for his food,
   Dares now range the wood;
But hushed in his lair he lies lurking:
   While mischiefs, by these,
   On land and on seas,
At noon of night are a-working.

   The storm will arise
   And trouble the skies;
This night, and more for the wonder,
   The ghost from the tomb
   Affrighted shall come,
Called out by the clap of the thunder.

Robert Herrick

from Witches' song

The owl is abroad, the bat and the toad,
  And so is the cat-a-mountain;
The ant and the mole sit both in a hole,
  And frog peeps out o' the fountain;
The dogs they do bay, and the timbrels play,
  The spindle is now a-turning;
The moon it is red, and the stars are fled,
  And all the sky is a-burning.

Ben Jonson

A charm

Bring the holy crust of bread,
Lay it underneath the head;
'Tis a certain charm to keep
Hags away, while children sleep.

Robert Herrick

A Cornish charm

From Ghosties and Ghoulies
And long-leggity Beasties,
And all things that go BUMP
in the night —
Good Lord, deliver us!

Unknown

Before sleeping

Matthew, Mark, Luke, and John,
Bless the bed that I lie on.
Before I lay me down to sleep
I give my soul to Christ to keep.
Four corners to my bed,
Four angels there aspread,
Two to foot and two to head,
And four to carry me when I'm dead.
I go by sea, I go by land,
The lord made me with His right hand.
If any danger come to me,
Sweet Jesus Christ deliver me.
He's the branch and I'm the flower,
Pray God send me a happy hour,
And if I die before I wake,
I pray that Christ my soul will take.

Unknown

from A goodnight

Close now thine eyes, and rest secure;
Thy soul is safe enough, thy body sure;
He that loves thee, He that keeps
And guards thee, never slumbers, never sleeps.

Francis Quarles

from Dream-pedlary

If there were dreams to sell,
    What would you buy?
Some cost a passing bell;
    Some a light sigh,
That shakes from Life's fresh crown
Only a rose-leaf down.
If there were dreams to sell,
Merry and sad to tell,
And the crier rang the bell,
    What would you buy?

Thomas Lovell Beddoes

85

Festivals and anniversaries

New Year carol

Here we bring new water
  from the well so clear,
For to worship God with,
  this happy New Year.
Sing levy dew, sing levy dew,
  the water and the wine;
The seven bright gold wires
  and the bugles that do shine.

Sing reign of Fair Maid
  with gold upon her toe –
Open you the West door,
  and turn the Old Year go.

Sing reign of Fair Maid
  with gold upon her chin –
Open you the East door,
  And let the Old Year in.
Sing levy dew, sing levy dew,
  the water and the wine;
The seven bright gold wires
  and the bugles that do shine.

Unknown

Epiphany

It was a king of Negro-land,
   A king of Chinatown,
And an old prince of Iran,
   Who to the Child kneeled down.

It was a king of blackamoors,
   A king of men slant-eyed,
A lord among sun-worshippers,
   Who at the New-born spied.

It was a king with savage eyes,
   King with a queer pigtail,
King with a high and sunlit brow,
   Who bade the New-born 'Hail!'

Back rode they to one country,
   One spiritual land,
Three kings of my soul's country
   Who touched the New-born's hand.

Charles Williams

Ceremony upon Candlemas Eve

Down with the rosemary, and so
Down with the bays and mistletoe;
Down with the holly, ivy, all
Wherewith ye dressed the Christmas hall;
That so the superstitious find
No one least branch there left behind;
For look, how many leaves there be
Neglected there, maids, trust to me,
So many goblins you shall see.

Robert Herrick

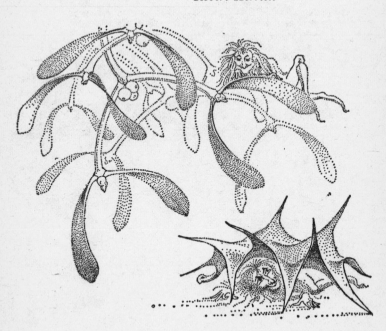

A charm for
St Valentine's Eve

I place my shoes like a letter T,
In hopes my true love I shall see,
In his apparel and his array,
As he is now and every day.

Unknown

Shrove Tuesday

Snick, snock, the pan's hot,
We be come a-shrovin'.
Please to gie us summat,
Summat's better'n nothin':
A bit o' bread, a bit o' cheese,
A bit o' apple dumplin' please.

Unknown

Pancakes

Mix a pancake,
Stir a pancake,
   Pop it in the pan;
Fry the pancake,
Toss the pancake,—
   Catch it if you can.

Christina Rossetti

The donkey

When fishes flew and forests walked
   And figs grew upon thorn,
Some moment when the moon was blood
   Then surely I was born;

With monstrous head and sickening cry
   And ears like errant wings,
The devil's walking parody
   On all four-footed things.

The tattered outlaw of the earth,
   Of ancient crooked will;
Starve, scourge, deride me: I am dumb,
   I keep my secret still.

Fools! For I also had my hour;
   One far fierce hour and sweet:
There was a shout about my ears,
   And palms before my feet.

G. K. Chesterton

Holy Thursday

'Twas on a Holy Thursday, their innocent faces clean,
Came children walking two and two, in red and blue and green,
Grey-headed beadles walked before, with wands as white as snow,
Till into the high dome of Paul's they like Thames' waters flow.

O what a multitude they seemed, these flowers of London town!
Seated in companies they sit with radiance all their own.
The hum of multitudes was there, but multitudes of lambs,
Thousands of little boys and girls raising their innocent hands.

Now, like a mighty wind they raise to Heaven the voice of song,
Or like harmonious thunderings the seats of Heaven among.
Beneath them sit the agèd men, wise guardians of the poor;
Then cherish pity, lest you drive an angel from your door.

William Blake

Easter

I got me flowers to straw Thy way,
  I got me boughs off many a tree;
But Thou wast up by break of day,
  And brought'st Thy sweets along with Thee.

Yet though my flowers be lost, they say
  A heart can never come too late;
Teach it to sing Thy praise this day,
  And then this day my life shall date.

George Herbert

He is risen

He is risen, he is risen,
  Tell it with a joyful voice;
He has burst his three days' prison;
  Let the whole wide earth rejoice.
Death is conquered, man is free,
Christ has won the victory.

C. F. Alexander

The world itself keeps Easter Day

The world itself keeps Easter Day,
The Easter larks are singing;
And Easter flowers are blooming gay,
And Easter buds are springing;
    Alleluya, Alleluya:
The Lord of all things lives anew,
And all His works are rising too.

There stood three Maries by the tomb,
On Easter morning early;
When day had scarcely chased the gloom,
And dew was white and pearly:
    Alleluya, Alleluya:
With loving but with erring mind,
They came the Prince of life to find.

The world itself keeps Easter Day,
Saint Joseph's Star is beaming;
Saint Alice has her primrose gay,
Saint George's Bells are gleaming;
    Alleluya, Alleluya:
The Lord hath risen, as all things tell:
Good Christians, see ye rise as well.

J. M. Neale

The first of April

The first of April, some do say,
Is set apart for All Fools' Day,
But why the people call it so
Nor I nor they themselves do know.

Unknown

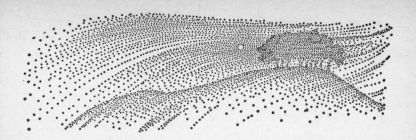

On May morning

Now the bright morning star, day's harbinger,
Comes dancing from the East, and leads with her
The flowery May, who from her green lap throws
The yellow cowslip, and the pale primrose.
  Hail, bounteous May! that dost inspire
  Mirth, and youth, and warm desire;
  Woods and groves are of thy dressing,
  Hill and dale doth boast thy blessing.
Thus we salute thee with our early song,
And welcome thee, and wish thee long.

John Milton

Haytime

It's Midsummer Day
And they're cutting the hay
Down in the meadow just over the way,
The children all run
For a frolic, and fun –
For haytime is playtime out in the sun.

It's Midsummer Day
And they're making the hay
Down in the meadow all golden and gay,
They're tossing it high
Beneath the June sky,
And the hay rakes are spreading it out to dry.

Irene F. Pawsey

from A Midsummer Night's Dream

Now the hungry lion roars,
   And the wolf behowls the moon;
Whilst the heavy ploughman snores,
   All with weary task fordone.
Now the wasted brands do glow,
   Whilst the screech-owl, screeching loud,
Puts the wretch that lies in woe
   In remembrance of a shroud.
Now it is the time of night
   That the graves, all gaping wide,
Every one lets forth his sprite,
   In the church-way paths to glide. . . .

William Shakespeare

Hallowe'en

This is the night when witches fly
On their whizzing broomsticks through the wintry sky;
Steering up the pathway where the stars are strewn,
They stretch skinny fingers to the waking moon.

This is the night when old wives tell
Strange and creepy stories, tales of charm and spell;
Peering at the pictures flaming in the fire
They wait for whispers from a ghostly choir.

This is the night when angels go
In and out the houses, winging o'er the snow;
Clearing out the demons from the countryside
They make it new and ready for Christmastide.

Leonard Clark

Hallowe'en

On Hallowe'en the old ghosts come
About us, and they speak to some;
To others they are dumb.

They haunt the hearts that loved them best;
In some they are by grief possessed,
In other hearts they rest.

They have a knowledge they would tell;
To some of us it is a knell,
To some, a miracle.

They come unseen and go unseen;
And some will never know they've been,
And some will know all they mean.

Eleanor Farjeon

The guy

Dogs break the dust
barking across the dark;
kids, shouting, crack
the air like ice,
ravaging wood or park,
log-laden, against the year's fall.

Shadowing street,
waste plot, or littered yard
they pile their tall
topheavy pyres
of branches, bent and tarred
to burn against this half-remembered ghost

as some straw Guy
who every year must flare
across the night,
fêted in fires,
flame-racked, yet unaware;
lapped in child's laughter endlessly.

Robert L. Holmes

Fireworks

They rise like sudden fiery flowers
That burst upon the night,
Then fall to earth in burning showers
Of crimson, blue and white.

Like buds too wonderful to name,
Each miracle unfolds,
And catherine-wheels begin to flame
Like whirling marigolds.

Rockets and roman-candles make
An orchard of the sky,
When magic trees their petals shake
Upon each gazing eye.

James Reeves

I sing of a maiden

I sing of a maiden
  That is makeless;
King of all kings
  To her son she ches.

He came all so still
  Where his mother was,
As dew in April
  That falleth on the grass.

He came all so still
  Where his mother lay,
As dew in April
  That falleth on the spray.

He came all so still
  To his mother's bower,
As dew in April
  That falleth on the flower.

Mother and maiden
  Was never none but she;
Well may such a maiden
  God's mother be.

                  Unknown

The holly and the ivy

The holly and the ivy,
When they are both full grown,
Of all the trees that are in the wood,
The holly bears the crown:

The rising of the sun
And the running of the deer,
The playing of the merry organ,
Sweet singing in the choir.

The holly bears a blossom,
As white as lily flower,
And Mary bore sweet Jesus Christ,
To be our sweet Saviour:

The holly bears a berry,
As red as any blood,
And Mary bore sweet Jesus Christ
To do poor sinners good:

The holly bears a prickle,
As sharp as any thorn,
And Mary bore sweet Jesus Christ
On Christmas day in the morn:

The holly bears a bark,
As bitter as any gall,
And Mary bore sweet Jesus Christ
For to redeem us all:

The holly and the ivy,
When they are both full grown,
Of all the trees that are in the wood,
The holly bears the crown.

Unknown

Chester carol

He who made the earth so fair
Slumbers in a stable bare,
Warmed by cattle standing there.

Oxen, lowing, stand all round;
In the stall no other sound
Mars the peace by Mary found.

Joseph piles the soft, sweet hay,
Starlight drives the dark away,
Angels sing a heavenly lay.

Jesus sleeps in Mary's arm;
Sheltered there from rude alarm,
None can do Him ill or harm.

See His mother o'er Him bend;
Hers the joy to soothe and tend,
Hers the bliss that knows no end.

Unknown
(From a Chester mystery play)

Moonless darkness
stands between

Moonless darkness stands between.
Past, O Past, no more be seen!
But the Bethlehem star may lead me
To the sight of Him who freed me
From the self that I have been.
Make me pure, Lord: Thou art holy;
Make me meek, Lord: Thou wert lowly;
Now beginning, and alway:
Now begin, on Christmas day.

Gerard Manley Hopkins

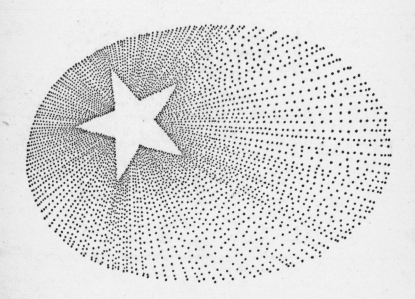

The Old Year

The Old Year's gone away
   To nothingness and night:
We cannot find him all the day
   Nor hear him in the night:
He left no footstep, mark or place
   In either shade or sun:
The last year he'd a neighbour's face,
   In this he's known by none.

All nothing everywhere:
   Mists we on mornings see
Have more of substance when they're here
   And more of form than he.
He was a friend by every fire,
   In every cot and hall –
A guest to every heart's desire,
   And now he's nought at all.

Old papers thrown away,
   Old garments cast aside,
The talk of yesterday,
   All things identified;
But times once torn away
   No voices can recall:
The eve of New Year's Day
   Left the Old Year lost to all.

John Clare

The twelve days of Christmas

On the twelfth day of Christmas
My true love sent to me
Twelve lords a-leaping,
Eleven ladies dancing,
Ten pipers piping,
Nine drummers drumming,
Eight maids a-milking,
Seven swans a-swimming,
Six geese a-laying,
Five gold rings,
Four colly birds,
Three French hens,
Two turtle-doves, and
A partridge in a pear-tree.

Unknown

Months and seasons

The garden year

January brings the snow,
Makes our feet and fingers glow.

February brings the rain,
Thaws the frozen lake again.

March brings breezes, loud and shrill,
To stir the dancing daffodil.

April brings the primrose sweet,
Scatters daisies at our feet.

May brings flocks of pretty lambs
Skipping by their fleecy dams.

June brings tulips, lilies, roses,
Fills the children's hands with posies.

Hot July brings cooling showers,
Apricots and gillyflowers.

August brings the sheaves of corn,
Then the harvest home is borne.

Warm September brings the fruit;
Sportsmen then begin to shoot.

Fresh October brings the pheasant;
Then to gather nuts is pleasant.

Dull November brings the blast;
Then the leaves are whirling fast.

Chill December brings the sleet,
Blazing fire, and Christmas treat.

Sara Coleridge

Last snow

Although the snow still lingers
Heaped on the ivy's blunt webbed fingers
And painted tree-trunks on one side,
Here in this sunlit ride
The fresh unchristened things appear,
Leaf, spathe and stem,
With crumbs of earth clinging to them
To show the way they came
But no flower yet to tell their name,
And one green spear
Stabbing a dead leaf from below
Kills winter at a blow.

Andrew Young

Spring

Already the slim crocus stirs the snow,
And soon the blanched fields will bloom again
With nodding cowslips for some lad to mow,
For with the first warm kisses of the rain
The winter's icy sorrow breaks to tears,
And the brown thrushes mate, and with bright eyes
      the rabbit peers
From the dark warren where the fir-cones lie,
And treads one snowdrop under foot, and runs
Over the mossy knoll.

             The blackbirds fly
Across our path at evening, and the suns
Stay longer with us; ah, how good to see
Grass-girdled Spring in all her joy of laughing
      greenery!

Oscar Wilde

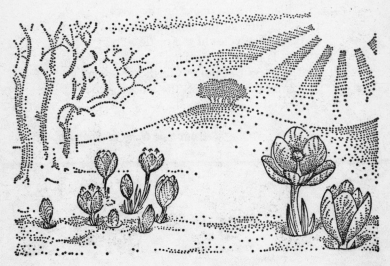

Thaw

Over the land freckled with snow half-thawed
The speculating rooks at their nests cawed
And saw from elm-tops, delicate as flower of grass,
What we below could not see, Winter pass.

Edward Thomas

The winter is past

For, lo, the winter is past,
The rain is over and gone;
The flowers appear on the earth;
The time of the singing of birds is come,
And the voice of the turtle
  Is heard in our land;
The fig-tree putteth forth her green figs,
And the vines with the tender grape
  Give a good smell.

from *The Song of Solomon*

Written in March

The cock is crowing,
The stream is flowing,
The small birds twitter,
The lake doth glitter,
The green field sleeps in the sun;
The oldest and youngest
Are at work with the strongest;
The cattle are grazing,
Their heads never raising;
There are forty feeding like one!

Like an army defeated
The snow hath retreated,
And now doth fare ill
On the top of the bare hill;
The ploughboy is whooping – anon – anon.
There's joy in the mountains;
There's life in the fountains;
Small clouds are sailing,
Blue sky prevailing;
The rain is over and gone!

William Wordsworth

Spring

Now the sleeping creatures waken –
   Waken, waken;
Blossoms with soft winds are shaken –
   Shaken, shaken;
Squirrels scamper and the hare
Runs races which the children share
Till their shouting fills the air.

Now the woodland birds are singing –
   Singing, singing;
Over field and orchard winging –
   Winging, winging;
Swift and swallow unaware
Weave such beauty on the air
That the children hush and stare.

Raymond Wilson

April day: Binsey

Now the year's let loose; it skips like a feckless child,
Ruffles our hair, rouses the trees, runs wild,
Kisses the hills with sunlight, whips them with rain,
Teases the grass in passing, gets lost in the lane.
Taut as lyre-strings the swan's wings quiver,
Lyre-strings plucked by the wind on the swollen river.
Shadows of clouds and cantering horses race
Over the meadows where heaven and earth embrace.

Michael Hamburger

The lark in the morning

As I was a-walking
One morning in spring,
I heard a pretty ploughboy,
So sweetly he did sing;
And as he was a-singing
These words I heard him say:
'Oh, there's no life like the ploughboy
All in the month of May.'

There's the lark in the morning
She will rise up from her nest,
She'll mount the white air
With the dew on her breast,
And with the pretty ploughboy O,
She'll whistle and she'll sing,
And at night she'll return
To her nest back again.

Unknown

Where the bee sucks

Where the bee sucks, there suck I,
In a cowslip's bell I lie,
There I couch when owls do cry;
On the bat's back I do fly
    After Summer merrily.
Merrily, merrily, shall I live now
Under the blossom that hangs on the bough.
                William Shakespeare

Summer

Winter is cold-hearted,
Spring is yea and nay,
Autumn is a weathercock
    Blown every way.
    Summer days for me
When every leaf is on its tree.

When Robin's not a beggar,
And Jenny Wren's a bride,
And larks hang singing, singing, singing,
    Over the wheat-fields wide,
    And anchored lilies ride,
    And the pendulum spider
    Swings from side to side;

And blue-black beetles transact business,
    And gnats fly in a host,
And furry caterpillars hasten
    That no time be lost,
    And moths grow fat and thrive,
    And ladybirds arrive.

Before green apples blush,
Before green nuts embrown,
Why, one day in the country
Is worth a month in town;
Is worth a day and a year
Of the dusty, musty, lag-last fashion
    That days drone elsewhere.

Christina Rossetti

from Amid the new-mown hay

When swallows dart from cottage eaves,
And farmers dream of barley sheaves;
When apples peep amid the leaves,
And wood-bines scent the way,
We love to fly from daily care,
To breathe the buxom country air,
To join our hands and form a ring.
To laugh and sport,
To dance and sing,
Amid the new-mown hay.

Charles MacKay

from Summer images

I love the south-west wind, or low or loud,
    And not the less when sudden drops of rain
Moisten my pallid cheek from ebon cloud,
    Threatening soft showers again,
That over lands new ploughed and meadow grounds,
    Summer's sweet breath unchain,
        And wake harmonious sounds.

Rich music breathes in summer's every sound;
    And in her harmony of varied greens,
Woods, meadows, hedge-rows, corn-fields, all around
    Much beauty intervenes,
Filling with harmony the ear and eye;
    While o'er the mingling scenes
        Far spreads the laughing sky.

John Clare

What could be lovelier than to hear

What could be lovelier than to hear
The summer rain
Cutting across the heat, as scythes
Cut across grain?
Falling upon the steaming roof
With sweet uproar,
Tapping and rapping wildly
At the door?

No, do not lift the latch,
But through the pane
We'll stand and watch the circus pageant
Of the rain,
And see the lightning, like a tiger,
Striped and dread,
And hear the thunder cross the sky
With elephant tread.

Elizabeth Coatsworth

Summer

Rushes in a watery place,
  And reeds in a hollow;
A soaring skylark in the sky,
  A darting swallow;
And where pale blossom used to hang
  Ripe fruit to follow.

Christina Rossetti

The wasp

When the ripe pears droop heavily,
The yellow wasp hums loud and long
His hot and drowsy summer song.
A yellow flame he seems to be,
When darting suddenly from high
He lights where fallen peaches lie.

Yellow and black – this tiny thing's
A tiger soul on elfin wings.

William Sharp

Harvest song

The boughs do shake and the bells do ring,
So merrily comes our harvest in,
Our harvest in, our harvest in,
So merrily comes our harvest in.

We have ploughed, we have sowed,
We have reaped, we have mowed,
We have brought home every load,
Hip, hip, hip, harvest home!

Unknown

Something told the wild geese

Something told the wild geese
It was time to go,
Though the fields lay golden
Something whispered, 'Snow!'
Leaves were green and stirring,
Berries lustre-glossed,
But beneath warm feathers
Something cautioned, 'Frost!'

All the sagging orchards
Steamed with amber spice,
But each wild beast stiffened
At remembered ice.
Something told the wild geese
It was time to fly –
Summer sun was on their wings,
Winter in their cry.

Rachel Field

Autumn

A touch of cold in the Autumn night—
I walked abroad,
And saw the ruddy moon lean over a hedge
Like a red-faced farmer.
I did not stop to speak, but nodded,
And round about were the wistful stars
With white faces like town children.

T. E. Hulme

Autumn song

There came a day that caught the summer
Wrung its neck
Plucked it
And ate it.

Now what shall I do with the sun?
The day said, the day said.
Strip them bare, strip them bare.
Let's see what is really there.

And what shall I do with the sun?
The day said, the day said.
Roll him away till he's cold and small.
He'll come back rested if he comes back at all.

And what shall I do with the birds?
The day said, the day said.
The birds I've frightened, let them flit,
I'll hang out pork for the brave tomtit.

And what shall I do with the seed?
The day said, the day said.
Bury it deep, see what it's worth.
See if it can stand the earth.

What shall I do with the people?
The day said, the day said.
Stuff them with apple and blackberry pie –
They'll love me then till the day they die.

There came this day and he was autumn.
His mouth was wide
And red as a sunset.
His tail was an icicle.

Ted Hughes

Sowing

It was a perfect day
For sowing: just
As sweet and dry was the ground
As tobacco-dust.

I tasted deep the hour
Between the far
Owl's chuckling first soft cry
And the first star.

A long stretched hour it was;
Nothing undone
Remained; the early seeds
All safely sown.

And now, hark at the rain,
Windless and light,
Half a kiss, half a tear,
Saying goodnight.

Edward Thomas

Autumn

I love the fitful gust that shakes
   The casement all the day,
And from the glossy elm tree takes
   The faded leaves away,
Twirling them by the window pane
With thousand others down the lane.

I love to see the shaking twig
   Dance till shut of eve,
The sparrow on the cottage rig,
   Whose chirp would make believe
That spring was just now flirting by
In Summer's lap with flowers to lie.

I love to see the cottage smoke
   Curl upwards through the trees;
The pigeons nestled round the cote
   On November days like these;
The cock upon the dunghill crowing,
The mill sails on the heath a-going.

John Clare

from A sheep fair

The day arrives of the autumn fair,
    And torrents fall,
Though sheep in throngs are gathered there,
    Ten thousand all,
Sodden, with hurdles round them reared:
And, lot by lot, the pens are cleared,
And the auctioneer wrings out his beard,
And wipes his book, bedrenched and smeared,
And rakes the rain from his face with the edge of his hand,
    As torrents fall.

Thomas Hardy

November night

Listen. . . .
With faint dry sound,
Like steps of passing ghosts,
The leaves, frost-crisped, break from the trees
And fall.

Adelaide Crapsey

Fall, leaves, fall

Fall, leaves, fall; die, flowers, away;
Lengthen night and shorten day;
Every leaf speaks bliss to me,
Fluttering from the autumn tree.

I shall smile when wreathes of snow
Blossom where the rose should grow;
I shall sing when night's decay
Ushers in a drearier day.

Emily Brontë

Beech leaves

In autumn down the beechwood path
  The leaves lie thick upon the ground.
It's there I love to kick my way
  And hear their crisp and crashing sound.

I am a giant, and my steps
  Echo and thunder to the sky.
How the small creatures of the woods
  Must quake and cower as I pass by!

This brave and merry noise I make
  In summer also when I stride
Down to the shining, pebbly sea
  And kick the frothing waves aside.

James Reeves

Winter the huntsman

Through his iron glades
Rides Winter the Huntsman.
All colour fades
As his horn is heard sighing.

Far through the forest
His wild hooves crash and thunder
Till many a mighty branch
Is torn asunder.

And the red reynard creeps
To his hole near the river,
The copper leaves fall
And the bare trees shiver.

As night creeps from the ground,
Hides each tree from its brother,
And each dying sound
Reveals yet another.

Is it Winter the Huntsman
Who gallops through his iron glades,
Cracking his cruel whip
To the gathering shades?

Osbert Sitwell

from Preludes

The winter evening settles down
With smell of steaks in passageways.
Six o'clock.
The burnt-out ends of smoky days.
And now a gusty shower wraps
The grimy scraps
Of withered leaves about your feet
And newspapers from vacant lots;
The showers beat
On broken blinds and chimney-pots,
And at the corner of the street
A lonely cab-horse steams and stamps.
And then the lighting of the lamps.

T. S. Eliot

Winter field

Sorrow on the acres,
Wind in the thorn,
And an old man ploughing
Through the frosty morn.

A flock of dark birds,
Rooks and their wives,
Follow the plough team
The old man drives;

And troops of starlings,
A-tittle-tat and prim,
Follow the rooks
That follow him.

A. E. Coppard

Winter

The frost is here,
The fuel is dear,
And woods are sear,
And fires burn clear,
And frost is here,
And has bitten the heel of the going year.

Bite, frost, bite!
You roll up away from the light,
The blue wood-louse and the plump dormouse,
And the bees are stilled and the flies are killed,
And you bite far into the heart of the house,
But not into mine.

Bite, frost, bite!
The woods are all the searer,
The fuel is all the dearer,
The fires are all the clearer,
My spring is all the nearer,
You have bitten into the heart of the earth,
But not into mine.

Alfred, Lord Tennyson

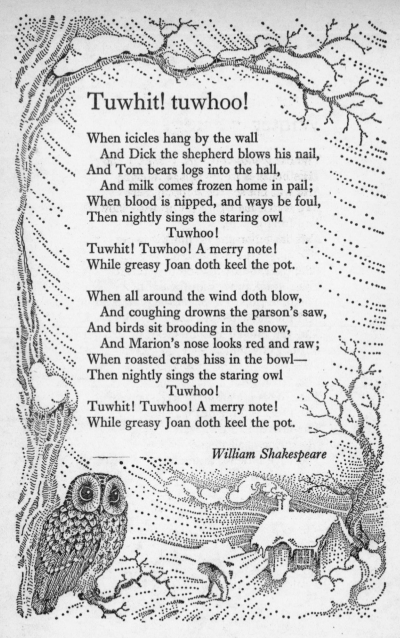

Tuwhit! tuwhoo!

When icicles hang by the wall
  And Dick the shepherd blows his nail,
And Tom bears logs into the hall,
  And milk comes frozen home in pail;
When blood is nipped, and ways be foul,
Then nightly sings the staring owl
          Tuwhoo!
Tuwhit! Tuwhoo! A merry note!
While greasy Joan doth keel the pot.

When all around the wind doth blow,
  And coughing drowns the parson's saw,
And birds sit brooding in the snow,
  And Marion's nose looks red and raw;
When roasted crabs hiss in the bowl—
Then nightly sings the staring owl
          Tuwhoo!
Tuwhit! Tuwhoo! A merry note!
While greasy Joan doth keel the pot.

William Shakespeare

Stopping by woods on a snowy evening

Whose woods these are I think I know.
His house is in the village though;
He will not see me stopping here
To watch his woods fill up with snow.

My little horse must think it queer
To stop without a farmhouse near
Between the woods and frozen lake
The darkest evening of the year.

He gives his harness bells a shake
To ask if there is some mistake.
The only other sound's the sweep
Of easy wind and downy flake.

The woods are lovely, dark and deep,
But I have promises to keep,
And miles to go before I sleep,
And miles to go before I sleep.

Robert Frost

The fallow deer at the lonely house

One without looks in tonight
   Through the curtain-chink
From the sheet of glistening white;
One without looks in tonight
   As we sit and think
   By the fender-brink.

We do not discern those eyes
   Watching in the snow;
Lit by lamps of rosy dyes
We do not discern those eyes
   Wondering, aglow,
   Fourfooted, tiptoe.

Thomas Hardy

January

The snow has melted now,
Uncovered on the lawn
The holly that we threw
Out when the year was done.
The crimson berries glow
Brilliant against the green,
And on a sculptured bough
Hard, black as ebony,
A robin-redbreast flings
Into the winter sky
His little sparks of song
Like promises of Spring.

Douglas Gibson

Time, you old Gipsy

To the virgins,
to make much of time

Gather ye rosebuds while ye may,
   Old Time is still a-flying:
And this same flower that smiles today
   Tomorrow will be dying.

The glorious lamp of heaven, the sun,
   The higher he's a-getting,
The sooner will his race be run,
   And nearer he's to setting.

That age is best which is the first,
   When youth and blood are warmer;
But being spent, the worse, and worst
   Times still succeed the former.

Then be not coy, but use your time,
   And while ye may, go marry:
For having lost but once your prime,
   You may for ever tarry.

Robert Herrick

It is not growing like a tree

It is not growing like a tree
In bulk, doth make men better be;
Or standing long an oak, three hundred year,
To fall a log at last, dry, bald, and sere:
A lily of a day
Is fairer far in May
Although it fall and die that night;
It was the plant and flower of light.
In small proportions we just beauties see;
And in short measures life may perfect be.

Ben Jonson

Lines written shortly before his execution

Even such is Time, that takes in trust
  Our youth, our joys, and all we have,
And pays us but with earth and dust;
  Who, in the dark and silent grave,
When we have wandered all our ways,
Shuts up the story of our days:
But from this earth, this grave, this dust,
My God shall raise me up, I trust.

Sir Walter Raleigh

Uphill

Does the road wind uphill all the way?
    Yes, to the very end.
Will the day's journey take the whole long day?
    From morn to night, my friend.

But is there for the night a resting-place?
  A roof for when the slow, dark hours begin.
May not the darkness hide it from my face?
  You cannot miss that inn.

Shall I meet other wayfarers at night?
  Those who have gone before.
Then must I knock, or call when just in sight?
  They will not keep you waiting at that door.

Shall I find comfort, travel-sore and weak?
  Of labour you shall find the sum.
Will there be beds for me and all who seek?
  Yea, beds for all who come.

Christina Rossetti

The traveller

Old man, old man, sitting on the stile,
Your boots are worn, your clothes are torn,
    Tell us why you smile.

Children, children, what silly things you are!
My boots are worn and my clothes are torn
    Because I've walked so far.

Old man, old man, where have you walked from?
Your legs are bent, your breath is spent –
    Which way did you come?

Children, children, when you're old and lame,
When your legs are bent and your breath is spent
    You'll know the way I came.

Old man, old man, have you far to go
Without a friend to your journey's end,
    And why are you so slow?

Children, children, I do the best I may:
I meet a friend at my journey's end
    With whom you'll meet some day.

Old man, old man, sitting on the stile,
How do you know which way to go,
    And why is it you smile?

Children, children, butter should be spread,
Floors should be swept and promises kept –
    And you should be in bed!

Raymond Wilson

The old men admiring themselves in the water

I heard the old, old men say,
'Everything alters,
And one by one we drop away.'
They had hands like claws, and their knees
Were twisted like the old thorn-trees
By the waters.
I heard the old men say,
'All that's beautiful drifts away
Like the waters.'

William Butler Yeats

Angler's song

Man's life is but vain, for 'tis subject to pain
And sorrow, and short as a bubble;
'Tis a hodgepodge of business, and money, and care,
And care, and money, and trouble.

But we'll take no care when the weather proves fair;
Nor will we vex though it rain;
We'll banish all sorrow, and sing till tomorrow
And angle and angle again.

Unknown

Like to the grass

Like to the grass that's newly sprung,
Or like a tale that's new begun,
Or like the bird that's here today,
Or like the pearlèd dew of May,
Or like an hour, or like a span,
Or like the singing of a swan –
Even such is man, who lives by breath,
Is here, now there: so life, and death.
The grass withers, the tale is ended,
The bird is flown, the dew's ascended,
The hour is short, the span not long,
The swan's near death; man's life is done.

Unknown

Time, you old Gipsy man

Time, you old Gipsy man,
  Will you not stay,
Put up your caravan
  Just for one day?

All things I'll give you,
Will you be my guest,
Bells for your jennet
Of silver the best,
Goldsmiths shall beat you
A great golden ring,
Peacocks shall bow to you,
Little boys sing,
Oh, and sweet girls will
Festoon you with may,
Time, you old gipsy,
Why hasten away?

Last week in Babylon,
Last night in Rome,
Morning, and in the crush
Under Paul's dome;
Under Paul's dial
You tighten your rein –
Only a moment,
And off once again;
Off to some city
Now blind in the womb,
Off to another
Ere that's in the tomb.

Time, you old gipsy man,
  Will you not stay,
Put up your caravan
  Just for one day?

                    Ralph Hodgson

154

All that's past

Very old are the woods;
And the buds that break
Out of the brier's boughs,
When March winds wake,
So old with their beauty are –
Oh, no man knows
Through what wild centuries
Roves back the rose.

Very old are the brooks;
And the rills that rise
Where snow sleeps cold beneath
The azure skies
Sing such a history
Of come and gone,
Their every drop is as wise
As Solomon.

Very old are we men;
Our dreams are tales
Told in dim Eden
By Eve's nightingales;
We wake and whisper awhile,
But, the day gone by,
Silence and sleep like fields
Of amaranth lie.

Walter de la Mare

The new house

Now first, as I shut the door,
    I was alone
In the new house; and the wind
    Began to moan.

Old at once was the house,
    And I was old;
My ears were teased with the dread
    Of what was foretold,

Nights of storm, days of mist, without end;
    Sad days when the sun
Shone in vain: old griefs and griefs
    Not yet begun.

All was foretold me; naught
    Could I foresee;
But I learned how the wind would sound
    After these things should be.

Edward Thomas

Robin's song

Robins sang in England,
   Frost or rain or snow,
All the long December days
   Endless years ago.

Robins sang in England
   Before the Legions came,
Before our English fields were tilled
   Or England was a name.

Robins sang in England
   When forests dark and wild
Stretched across from sea to sea
   And Jesus was a child.

Listen! in the frosty dawn
   From his leafless bough
The same brave song he ever sang
   A robin's singing now.

Rodney Bennett

On Wenlock Edge

On Wenlock Edge the wood's in trouble;
His forest fleece the Wrekin heaves;
The gale, it plies the saplings double,
And thick on Severn snow the leaves.

'Twould blow like this through holt and hanger
When Uricon the city stood:
'Tis the old wind in the old anger,
But then it threshed another wood.

Then, 'twas before my time, the Roman
At yonder heaving hill would stare:
The blood that warms an English yeoman,
The thoughts that hurt him, they were there.

There, like the wind through woods in riot,
Through him the gale of life blew high;
The tree of man was never quiet:
Then 'twas the Roman, now 'tis I.

The gale, it plies the saplings double,
It blows so hard, 'twill soon be gone.
To-day the Roman and his trouble
Are ashes under Uricon.

A. E. Housman

Gone

Where's the Queen of Sheba?
Where King Solomon?
Gone with Boy Blue who looks after the sheep,
Gone and gone and gone.

Lovely is the sunshine;
Lovely is the wheat;
Lovely the wind from out of the clouds
Having its way with it.

Rise up, Old Green-Stalks!
Delve deep, Old Corn!
But where's the Queen of Sheba?
Where King Solomon?

Walter de la Mare

A prehistoric camp

It was the time of year
   Pale lambs leap with thick leggings on
Over small hills that are not there,
   That I climbed Eggardon.

The hedgerows still were bare,
   None ever knew so late a year;
Birds built their nests in the open air,
   Love conquering their fear.

But there on the hill-crest,
   Where only larks or stars look down,
Earthworks exposed a vaster nest,
   Its race of men long flown.

Andrew Young

Egypt's might is tumbled down

Egypt's might is tumbled down
   Down a-down the deeps of thought;
Greece is fallen and Troy town,
Glorious Rome hath lost her crown,
     Venice' pride is nought.

But the dreams their children dreamed
   Fleeting, unsubstantial, vain,
Shadowy as the shadows seemed,
Airy nothing, as they deemed,
     These remain.

Mary Coleridge

The song of the mad prince

Who said, 'Peacock Pie'?
  The old King to the sparrow:
Who said, 'Crops are ripe'?
  Rust to the harrow:
Who said, 'Where sleeps she now?
  Where rests she now her head,
Bathed in eve's loveliness'?—
  That's what I said.

Who said, 'Ay, mum's the word'?
  Sexton to willow:
Who said, 'Green dusk for dreams,
  Moss for a pillow'?
Who said, 'All Time's delight
  Hath she for narrow bed;
Life's troubled bubble broken'?—
  That's what I said.

Walter de la Mare

Index of first lines

O summer sun, O moving trees! *15*
O why do you walk through the fields in gloves *13*
Old man, old man, sitting on the stile *150*
On Hallowe'en the old ghosts come *102*
On his little twig of plum *30*
On moony nights the dogs bark shrill *62*
On the twelfth day of Christmas *110*
On Wenlock Edge the wood's in trouble *158*
One without looks in tonight *144*
Out of the bosom of the air *49*
Over the land freckled with snow half-thawed *116*

Robins sang in England *157*
Rounding the corner *74*
Rushes in a watery place *125*

Sister, awake! close not your eyes *71*
Snick, snock, the pan's hot *91*
Something told the wild geese *128*
Sorrow on the acres *140*
Subtle as an illusionist *33*
Sweet Chance, that led my steps abroad *13*

The boughs do shake and the bells do ring *127*
The cock is crowing *117*
The day arrives of the autumn fair *134*
The first of April, some do say *96*
The first snow was sleet. It swished heavily *49*
The fog comes *46*
The frost is here *141*
The glass is going down *32*
The Hag is astride *82*
The holly and the ivy *106*
The key turns in the lock *81*
The midday hour of twelve the clock counts o'er *58*
The moon on the one hand, the dawn on the other *10*

Index of authors

More Beaver Books

We hope you have enjoyed this Beaver Book. Here are some of the other titles:

The City of Gold and Lead The second book of John Christopher's outstanding 'Tripods' trilogy, about the struggle to overthrow the Masters, invaders from outer space. The first book is *The White Mountains* and the third *The Pool of Fire*, both published in Beavers

When Darkness Comes A primitive tribe struggles for survival when torn apart by internal rivalries, but the appearance of a strange enemy makes unity essential. Robert Swindells has written a powerful first novel for older children

The Worst Kids in the World The Sunday school Christmas pageant turned out to be very different from usual the year the Herdmans bagged all the star parts. Judith Gwyn Brown's illustrations accompany Barbara Robinson's funny yet sensitive story

White Fang Jack London's great classic story about the life of a wild wolf dog at the time of the Gold Rush in the Yukon

Picture Puzzles Ninety-six pages packed with a variety of brain-teasers, including mazes, 'spot-the-difference' and 'I spy' games, written and illustrated by Walter Shepherd

Caring for a Horse or Pony The second of four titles in the Young Riders Guides series. This series gives all the information the young enthusiast needs to know about buying and keeping a horse or pony, caring for its health, feeding, riding and jumping. Written by Robert Owen and John Bullock, illustrated throughout with line drawings and black and white photographs

New Beavers are published every month and if you would like the *Beaver Bulletin* – which gives all the details – please send a large stamped envelope to:

Beaver Bulletin
The Hamlyn Group
Astronaut House
Feltham
Middlesex TW14 9AR

37128X